**Mensa** KiDS

TRAIN your BRAIN

PUZZLE BOOK

CRANIUM CRUNCHERS

THIS IS A CARLTON BOOK

Text, design and artwork copyright © Carlton Books Limited 2016

This edition published in 2016 by Carlton Books Limited
An imprint of the Carlton Publishing Group
20 Mortimer Street, London, W1T 3JW

10 9 8 7 6 5 4 3 2 1

A catalogue record for this book is available from the British Library.

ISBN 978-1-78312-193-9

Printed in Dongguan, China

Editor: Tasha Percy
Designed by: Alison Tutton
Art Editor: Dani Lurie
Production: Lisa Cook

Mensa® KiDS

TRAIN your BRAIN

PUZZLE BOOK

CRANIUM CRUNCHERS

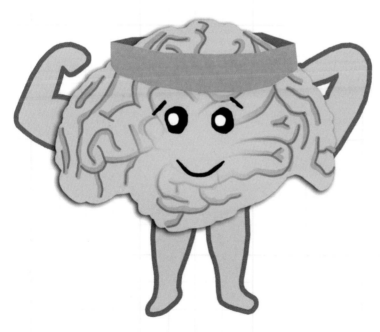

CARLTON KiDS

INTRODUCTION

THIS PUZZLE BOOK WILL TRAIN YOUR BRAIN IN NO TIME.

Are you ready to challenge your brain? This book is packed from cover to cover with a huge range of puzzles and tasks to test your thinking skills and your mental abilities!

The book is divided into three skill levels, with lots of puzzles at each level. You should start with Level A, then work your way up to Level B and then finally Level C – the challenges get harder at every stage!

All you need to solve any puzzle is your brain – and occasionally a pencil. Most of the puzzles can be solved without writing in the book, but there are just a few where you'll need to make some notes on the page, or copy the puzzle out if you're sharing this book with other people.

There are solutions at the back of the book so you can check your answers, or take a cheeky look if you get really stuck! But you won't do that, will you?

Lets get started!

READY TO GET THAT BRAIN BUZZING?

WHAT IS MENSA?

Mensa is the international society for people with a high IQ. We have more than 100,000 members in over 40 countries worldwide. The society's aims are:

* To identify and foster human intelligence for the benefit of humanity

* To encourage research in the nature, characteristics, and uses of intelligence

* To provide a stimulating intellectual and social environment for its members.

Anyone with an IQ score in the top two per cent of the population is eligible to become a member of Mensa – are you the 'one in 50' we've been looking for? Mensa membership offers an excellent range of benefits:

* Networking and social activities nationally and around the world
* Special Interest Groups – hundreds of chances to pursue your hobbies and interests – from art to zoology!
* Monthly members' magazine and regional newsletters
* Local meetings – from games challenges to food and drink
* National and international weekend gatherings and conferences
* Intellectually stimulating lectures and seminars
* Access to the worldwide SIGHT network for travellers and hosts.

For more information about Mensa:
www.mensa.org.uk
Telephone: +44 (O) 1902 772771
Email: services@mensa.org.uk
British Mensa Ltd, St John's House, St John's Square,
Wolverhampton WV2 4AH

PUZZLE 1

Arrange the numbers and maths symbols in each set so that they result in the given number. For example, in the first set you could make 6 with 1 x 4 + 2.

A $\boxed{1}\ \boxed{2}\ \boxed{4}\ \boxed{+}\ \boxed{\times}\ \boxed{=}\ \boxed{9}$

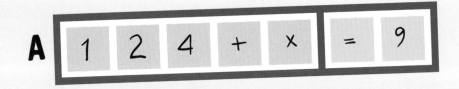

B $\boxed{2}\ \boxed{3}\ \boxed{3}\ \boxed{+}\ \boxed{\times}\ \boxed{=}\ \boxed{12}$

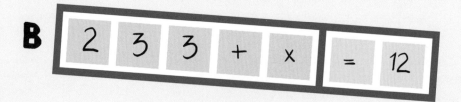

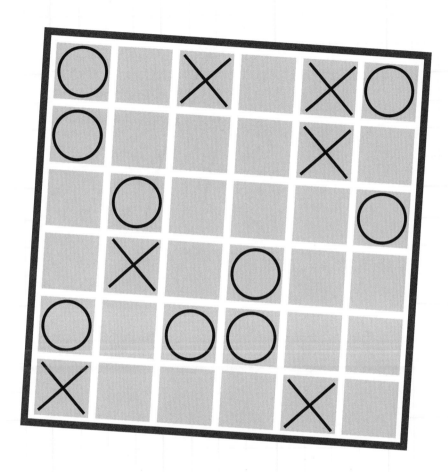

PUZZLE 2

Place either an X or an O in every empty square of this grid, without making any horizontal, vertical or diagonal lines of four or more Xs or Os!

PUZZLE 3

By picking one number from each of the three rings of this dartboard, can you make each of the following totals? For example, you could make a total of 36 by picking 11 from the innermost ring, 12 from the middle ring, and 13 from the outermost ring.

14   23   30

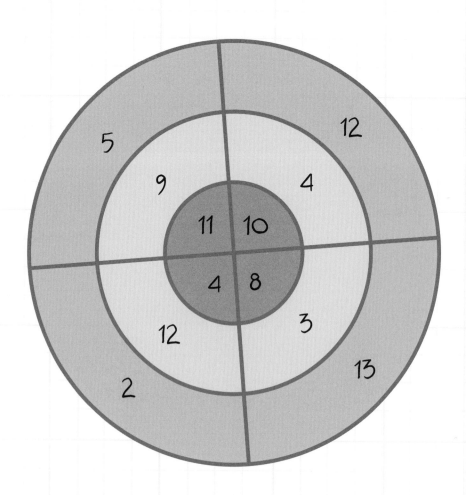

PUZZLE 4

Which number comes next in the following sequence?

3	5	8	12	17	23	?

PUZZLE 5

Each brick in this pyramid contains a number equal to the sum of the two bricks immediately below it, although some numbers are hidden. Can you work out the number that should be on the very top brick of the pyramid, marked with a bold question mark?

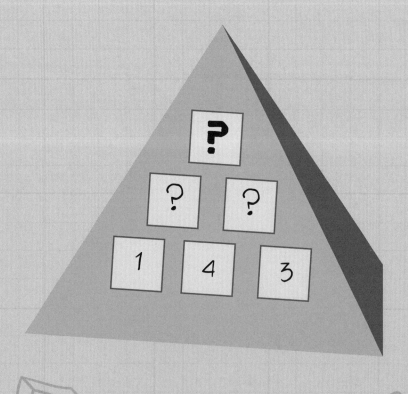

R B C Q A O P T N Z S Y G D U E I K W H J X F L M

PUZZLE 6

Every letter of the alphabet, A to Z, appears in this picture except for one — which letter is missing?

PUZZLE 7

Look at this set of letters for 30 seconds, then cover them with a piece of paper or another book. Now write out as many as you can remember on a separate piece of paper. Once you've done that, uncover the page again and see how many you remembered correctly.

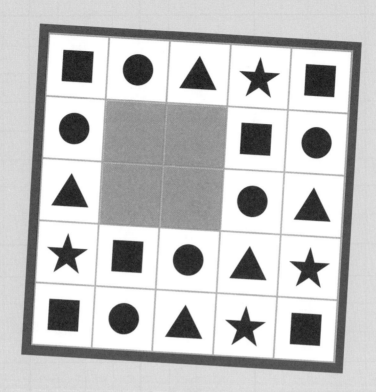

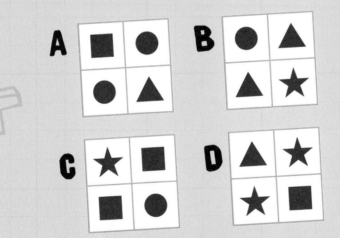

PUZZLE 8

Which of the options, A, B, C or D, can replace
the shaded area to complete the pattern?

PUZZLE 9

How many cubes can you count in this drawing? Don't forget to count the 'hidden' ones at the back that must be holding up the cubes above them!

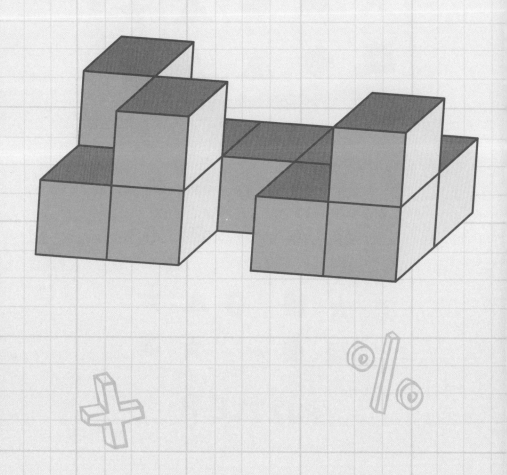

PUZZLE 10

In Puzzleland, there are coins of six different values:
1p, 2p, 5p, 10p, 20p and 50p.

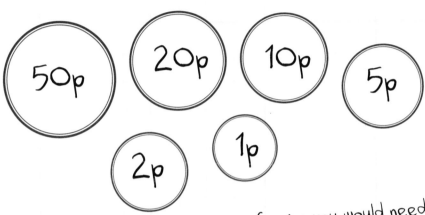

What is the smallest number of coins you would need
to buy each of the following things, without getting
any change:

A A ruler that costs 8p?

B A pencil case that costs 37p?

PUZZLE 11

Which of the options, A, B or C, can replace the
question mark to perfectly balance the bottom scale?

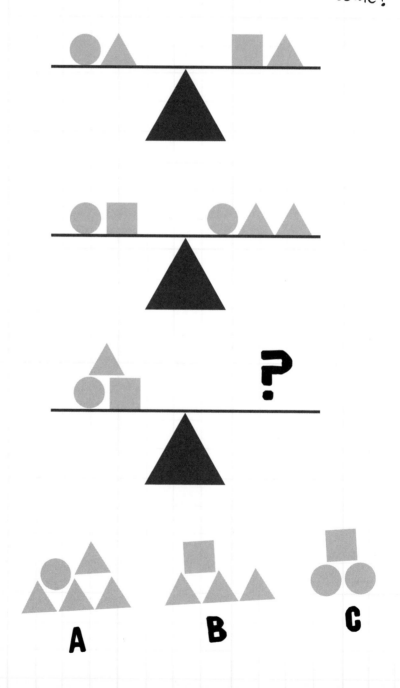

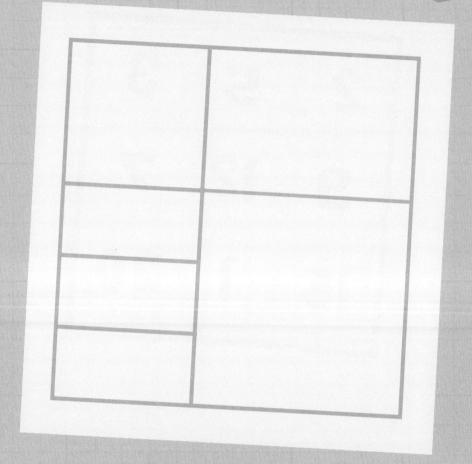

PUZZLE 12

How many rectangles and squares, of any size, can you count in this picture? Some are tricky to spot!

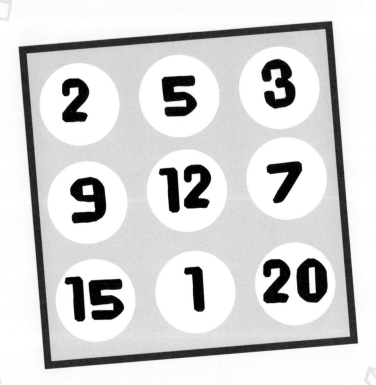

PUZZLE 13

Look at this list of numbers for 30 seconds, then cover them with a piece of paper or another book. Now write out as many as you can remember on a separate piece of paper. Once you've done that, uncover the page again and see how many you remembered correctly.

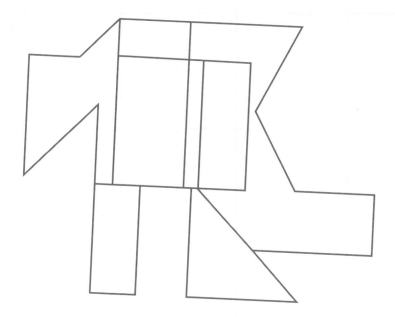

PUZZLE 14

Which of the shadows, A to D, exactly matches the outline of the larger shape at the top of the page? The shadows are all rotated and a bit smaller, just to make it trickier!

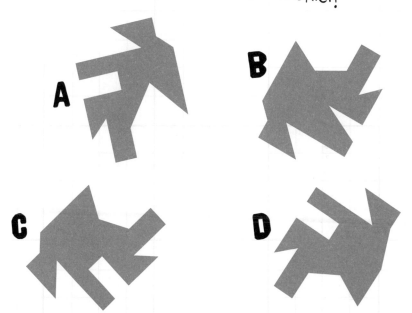

PUZZLE 15

How quickly can you solve this Brain Chain? Start with the number on the left, then apply each maths operation in turn. What is the final result?

| 19 | +18 | -19 | ÷3 | +17 | -18 | ? |

THINK HARD!

PUZZLE 16

Can you find your way through this maze, without drawing on the page? Enter through the gap at the top, and exit through the gap at the bottom.

Entrance

Exit

PUZZLE 17

Imagine drawing along the grid lines — can you work out how to divide this picture up into four identical shapes? Each grid square forms part of one of the four shapes, and none of the shapes overlap. You can rotate the shapes so they look the same, but you can't flip them.

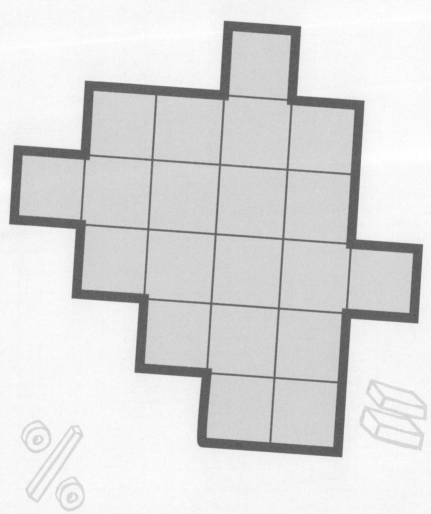

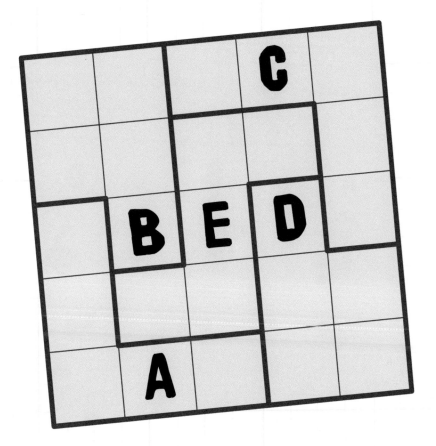

PUZZLE 18

Fill every empty square with a letter from A to E,
so that each row, column and bold-lined shape
contains each letter exactly once.

PUZZLE 19

If you were to rotate each image, A to C, by its corresponding arrow, which of the options 1 to 3 would result in each case? In other words, rotate image A by 90 degrees clockwise; rotate image B by 180 degrees; and rotate image C by 90 degrees anticlockwise.

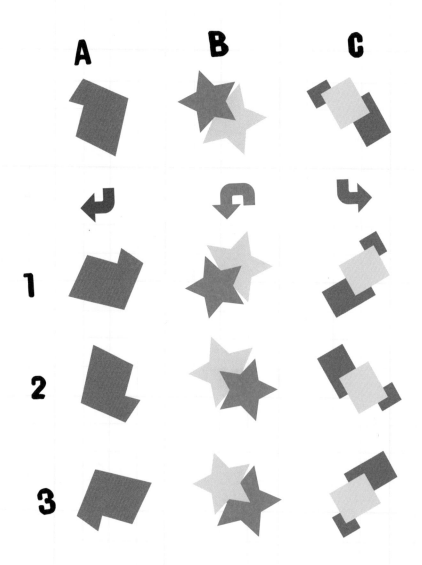

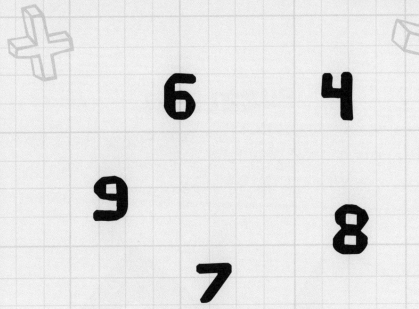

PUZZLE 20

By adding together two or more of these floating numbers, can you make all of the different totals below? Each floating number can only be used once per total.

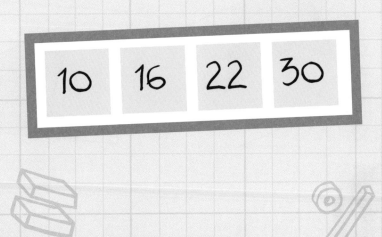

PUZZLE 21

Imagine cutting out and then rearranging these tiles into a 2 x 2 grid, to reveal a solid shape.
What shape would be revealed?

PUZZLE 22

You have two normal six-sided dice. Roll them both and then add the numbers together. There are two ways you could roll a total of 3: 2 and 1 or 1 and 2.

How many ways are there to roll a total of 7?

How many ways are there to roll a total of 4?

PUZZLE 23

Look at this set of shapes for 30 seconds, then cover them with a piece of paper or another book. Now draw out as many as you can remember on a separate piece of paper, in the same order. Once you've done that, uncover the page again and see how many you remembered both correctly and in the correct position.

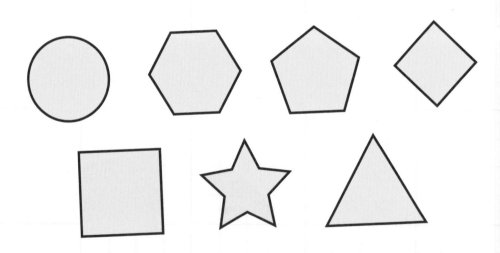

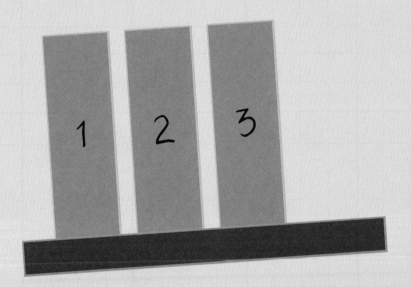

PUZZLE 24

Three books are arranged on a shelf, as shown. Can you work out which book is in each position?

* Driving Cars is to the left of Baking For Fun.

* All About Me is to the right of Driving Cars.

* Baking For Fun is on one end of the row.

PUZZLE 25

Most, but not all, of these boxes contain different sets of shapes. How many pairs of boxes containing identical symbols can you find?

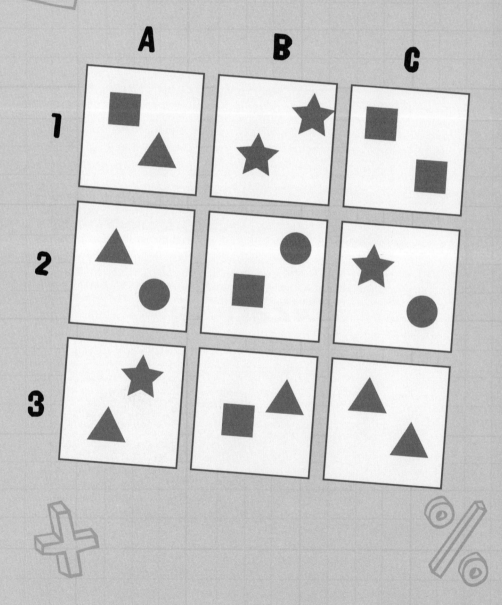

PUZZLE 26

Can you work out the hidden relationship that should replace the question mark in the centre? It transforms each number into its directly opposite number, following the direction of the arrows.

WORK THOSE CELLS!

PUZZLE 27

Here are the six faces of a standard pink dice:

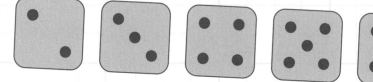

Some dots have rubbed off these white dice, so you can't be sure what number each side shows:

A What is the highest total value that these four sides could add up to?

B And what is the lowest total value that these four sides could add up to?

PUZZLE 28

Can you work out what shape would be revealed if you were to draw lines to join up all of the odd-numbered dots in numerical order, starting at the lowest and finishing at the highest?

11

13

6

16

8

9

15

2

4

12

10

7

18

17

14

5

3 19

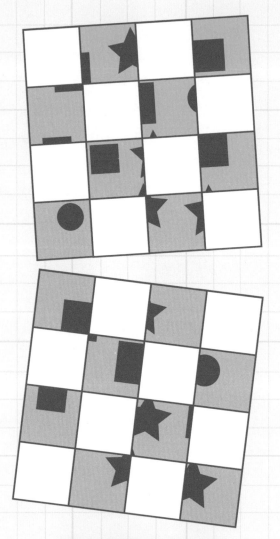

PUZZLE 29

The picture above is shown twice, but in each case different parts of it are covered with white squares. Imagine combining both images to see the complete picture. Can you count how many stars there are, how many squares there are, and how many circles there are?

LEVEL B: MEGA MIND

PUZZLE 30

Look at the following list of words for 30 seconds, then cover them with a piece of paper or another book. Now write out as many as you can remember on a separate piece of paper. Once you've done that, uncover the page again and see how many you remembered correctly.

ANT

MONKEY

DOUGHNUT

PEACOCK

NOBODY

RULER

SUN

ZOO

PUZZLE 31

Look closely at each picture, 1, 2 and 3. Can you work out which option, A, B or C, would be each of the picture's mirror-image reflection across the horizontal line?

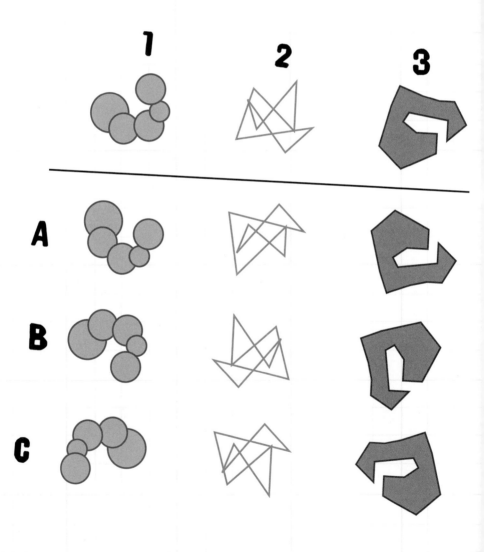

PUZZLE 32

Can you work out the numbers that should replace the question marks in the centre? They transform each number into its directly opposite number, following the direction of the arrows. This puzzle has two steps — first you multiply, then you add.

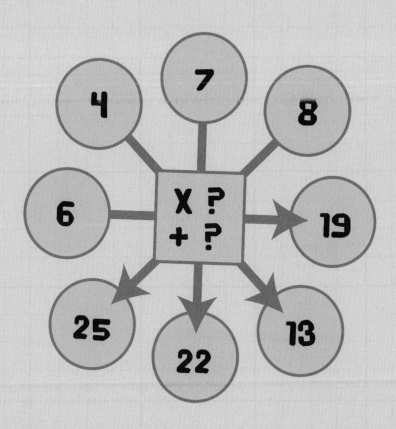

PUZZLE 33

By adding together two or more of these floating numbers, can you make all of the different totals below? Each floating number can only be used once per total.

8

17

11

10

18

16

| 24 | 33 | 42 | 55 |

PUZZLE 34

Draw lines in the grid to connect each pair of identical shapes, as in this example:

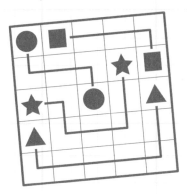

Lines can't cross or touch each other, and only one line is allowed in each grid square. Diagonal lines aren't allowed. Now solve this puzzle:

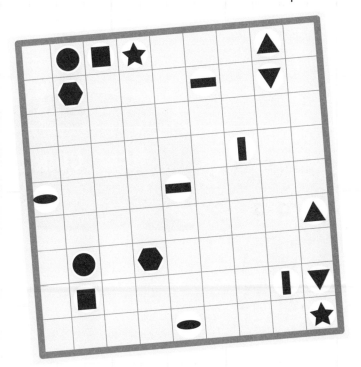

PUZZLE 35

How quickly can you solve this Brain Chain?
Start with the number on the left, then apply
each maths operation in turn. What is the
final result?

7 > +11 > x⅙ > x8 > ÷6 > +1 > ?

KEEP GOING!

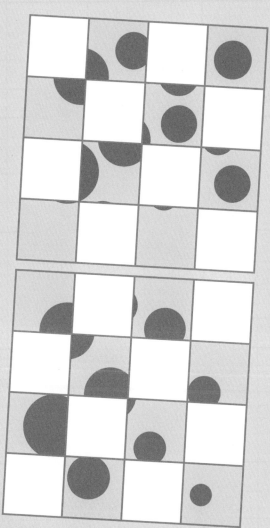

PUZZLE 36

The picture above is shown twice, but in each case different parts of it are covered with white squares. Imagine combining both images to see the complete picture. Can you count how many circles there are in total?

PUZZLE 37

Which number comes next in the following sequence?

| 2 | 4 | 8 | 16 | 32 | 64 | 128 | ? |

THIS IS A GREAT WORKOUT!

PUZZLE 38

Can you complete this domino chain? Each of the separate dominoes at the bottom of the page fits into one of the shaded domino positions. When complete, all touching dominoes should have the same number of dots on their touching halves.

PUZZLE 39

Look at this first set of shapes for 30 seconds, then cover just this first set with a piece of paper or another book:

Now look at the second set below – this contains the same shapes, but in a different order. Using a separate piece of paper, can you draw the shapes in the same order as the first set? Check your answer – how many did you get in the correct position?

PUZZLE 40

In Puzzleland, there are coins of six different values: 1p, 2p, 5p, 10p, 20p and 50p.

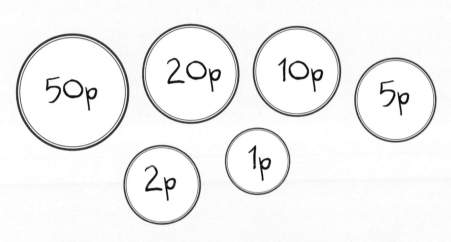

A What is the maximum price you can pay for something without using any coin more than once?

B You buy something that costs 66p using two 50p coins. What is the smallest number of coins you can receive back if you are given the exact change?

PUZZLE 41

Can you find your way through this circular maze, entering at the top and exiting at the bottom?

Entrance

Exit

PUZZLE 42

Which shape is the odd one out, and why?

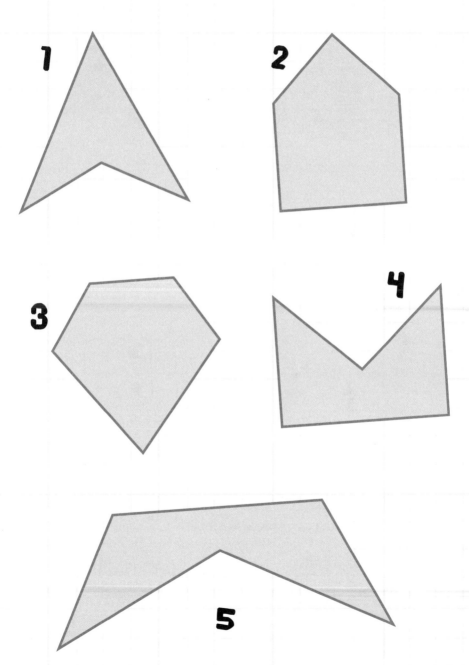

PUZZLE 43

Here are the six faces of a standard yellow dice:

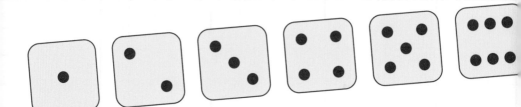

Some dots have rubbed off these white dice, so you can't be sure what number each side shows:

A What is the highest total value that these five sides could add up to?

B And what is the lowest total value that these five sides could add up to?

PUZZLE 44

Look at this first list of letters for 30 seconds, then cover just this first list with a piece of paper or another book:

H A T P S I E F W L C

Now look at the second list below – this contains the same letters, but in a different order. Using a separate piece of paper, can you rewrite the letters in the same order as the first list? Check your answer – how many did you get in the correct position?

A C E F H I L P S T W

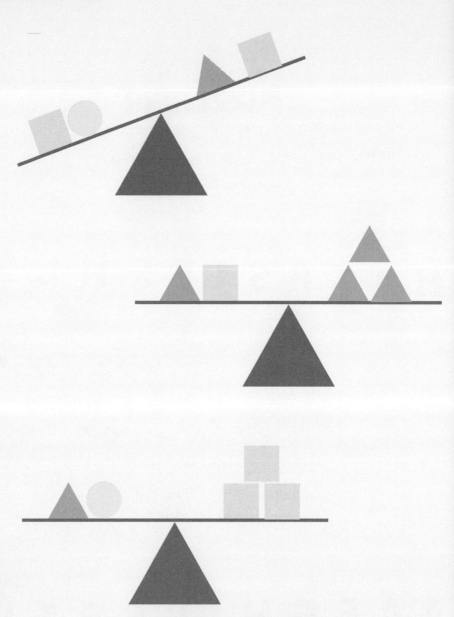

PUZZLE 45

Each shape is a different weight. Which is the heaviest shape, and which is the lightest shape?

PUZZLE 46

Reveal the hidden mines! Each number in the grid tells you how many of the touching squares, including diagonally touching squares, contain mines. None of the numbered squares contain mines themselves, however. Shade in a square if you know it doesn't contain a mine. Put an X in it if it does.

	2				1
0			5	3	1
	3	5		2	0
2				4	1
	3	4			2
		1	2		

PUZZLE 47

Arrange the numbers and maths symbols in each set so that they result in the given number. For example, in the first set you could make 7 with 2 x 2 + 2 + 1.

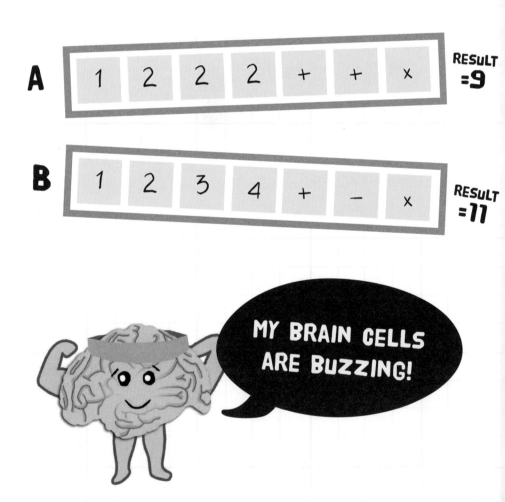

A | 1 | 2 | 2 | 2 | + | + | x | RESULT =9

B | 1 | 2 | 3 | 4 | + | − | x | RESULT =11

MY BRAIN CELLS ARE BUZZING!

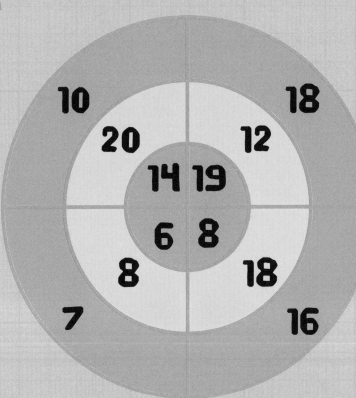

PUZZLE 48

By picking one number from each of the three rings of this dartboard, can you make each of the following totals? For example, you could make a total of 31 by picking 6 from the innermost ring, 18 from the middle ring, and 7 from the outermost ring.

29   39   48

PUZZLE 49

Imagine cutting out and then rearranging these tiles
into a 2 x 3 grid, to reveal a solid shape.
How many sides would it have?

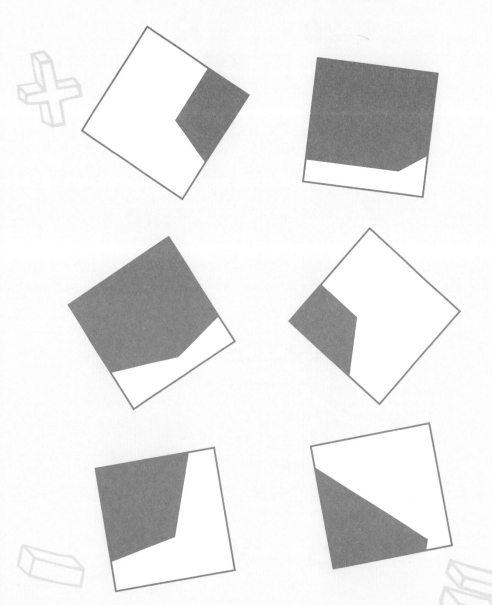

PUZZLE 50

Write a letter from A to F in each empty square, so that no letter is repeated in any row or column. Identical letters can't touch one another – not even diagonally.

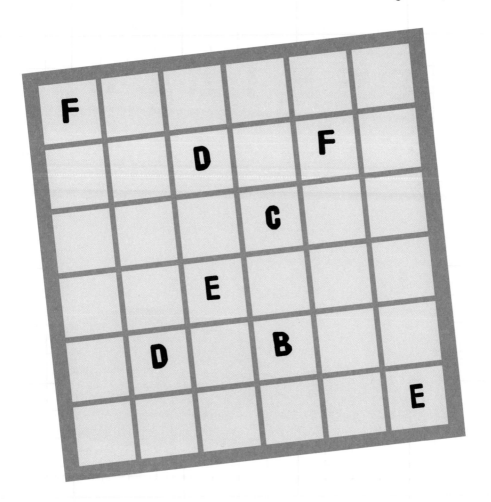

PUZZLE 51

Can you work out which letter comes next in this sequence?

A E F H I K L M ?

PUZZLE 52

Complete this 8x8 Sudoku puzzle by placing a number from one to eight in each empty square. Place the numbers so that no number repeats in any row, column or bold-lined box.

			1	2			
	2	3			5	7	
	1	7			6	4	
3							2
1							6
	7	2			3	1	
	5	8			2	3	
			7	4			

PUZZLE 53

All of these numbers appear twice except for one, which appears three times. Which number is that?

12 14 32 23
18
20 33 11 12 15
32 19 15 22
19 16
22 23 20 33
16 28 22 18 28
27 11 14 27

PUZZLE 54

You walk for 5 minutes, then ride a train for twice as long as that. You then get off the train and walk for half an hour. What is the total length of time your journey has taken?

YOU'RE GETTING GOOD AT THIS!

PUZZLE 55

Which of the options, A, B, C or D, can replace the shaded area to complete the pattern?

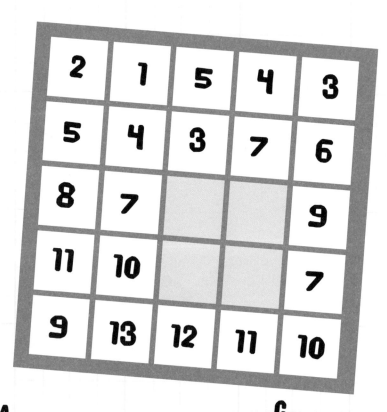

A

6	5
9	8

B

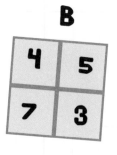

4	5
7	3

C

8	9
1	4

D

1	10
4	8

PUZZLE 56

All but one of these shapes can be cut out and then folded along the lines to make a perfect six-sided cube. Without actually cutting them out, can you work out which is the odd one out?

PUZZLE 57

Can you add or subtract all of these times?
The first row is done for you as an example.

13:30 + 07:15 = **20:45**   20:10 – 07:10 = **13:00**

16:40 + 02:45 =   09:20 – 02:30 =

23:10 – 14:05 =   03:25 – 02:15 =

17:30 – 08:15 =   10:40 + 10:00 =

21:30 – 20:30 =   04:05 + 05:05 =

00:15 + 06:30 =   18:55 – 07:25 =

08:25 – 02:00 =   15:30 + 04:00 =

09:45 – 00:05 =   01:15 + 05:00 =

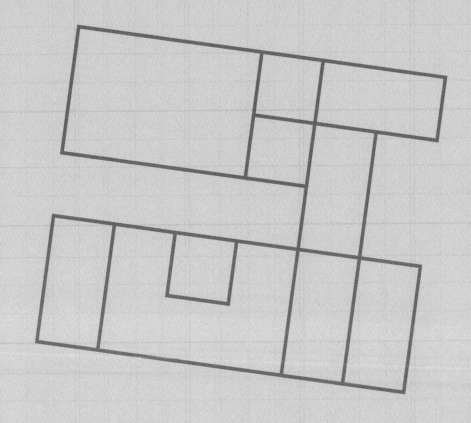

PUZZLE 58

How many rectangles and squares, of any size, can you count in this picture? Some are tricky to spot!

LEVEL C: ULTRA GENIUS

PUZZLE 59

Arrange the numbers and maths symbols in each set
so that they result in the given number.
For example, in the first set you could make
10 with 2 × 4 + 7 − 5.

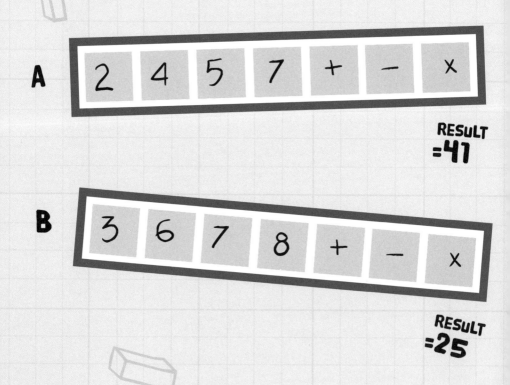

A

| 2 | 4 | 5 | 7 | + | − | × |

RESULT =41

B

| 3 | 6 | 7 | 8 | + | − | × |

RESULT =25

PUZZLE 60

Place either an X or an O in every empty square of
this grid, without making any horizontal, vertical or
diagonal lines of four or more Xs or Os!

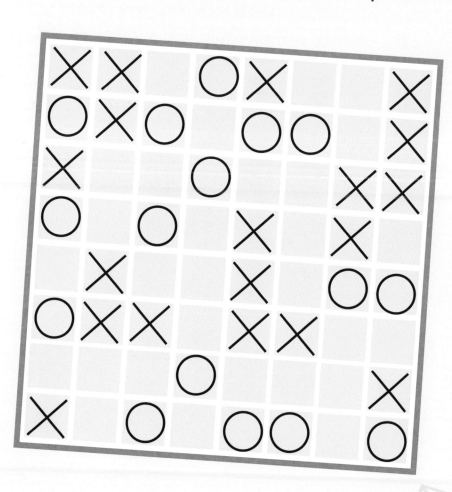

PUZZLE 61

Each brick in this pyramid contains a number equal to the sum of the two bricks immediately below it, although some numbers are hidden. Can you work out the numbers that should be on the very top brick of the pyramid, marked with a bold question mark?

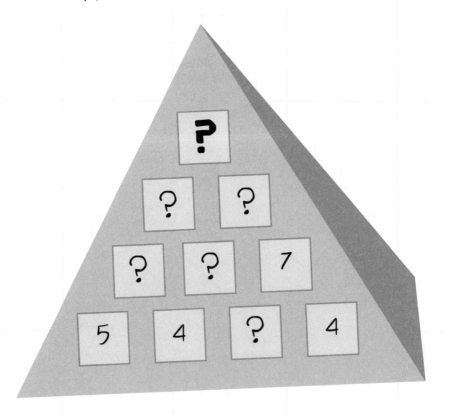

PUZZLE 62

Which number comes next in the following sequence?

| 1 | 1 | 2 | 3 | 5 | 8 | 13 | 21 | 34 | ? |

UP AND AT IT!

PUZZLE 63

Every letter of the alphabet, A to Z, appears twice in this picture except for one, which appears three times – which letter is that?

B R C U F G E P
H S P V Q Z I K
S U T Q Y G R D
C L O N H V A K
W E J Z M N J
D B I X L F M
X H T A W O Y

PUZZLE 64

How many rectangles and squares, of any size, can you count in this picture? Some are tricky to spot!

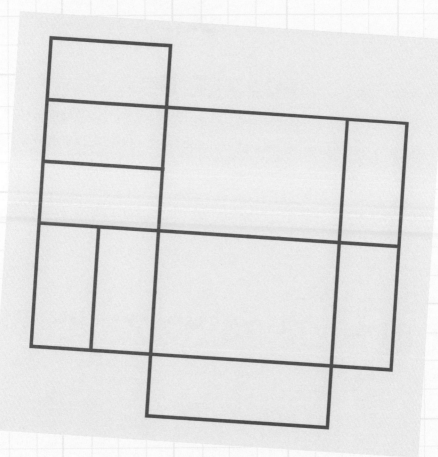

PUZZLE 65

Look at this set of numbers for 30 seconds, then cover them with a piece of paper or another book. Now write out as many as you can remember on a separate piece of paper. Once you've done that, uncover the page and see how many you remembered correctly.

11 91 51 13 73 43 77 44 33

PUZZLE 66

Can you work out which letter comes next in the following sequence? Here's a clue: think about numbers!

O T T F F S S E ?

I KNOW THIS ONE!

PUZZLE 67

Which of the shadows, A to D, exactly matches the outline of the larger shape at the top of the page? The shadows are all rotated and a bit smaller, just to make it trickier!

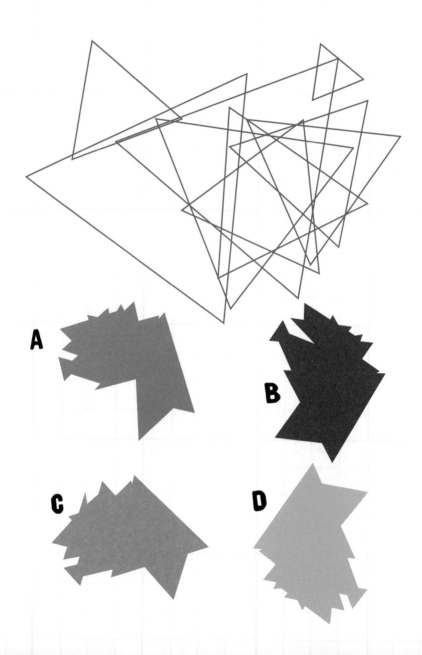

PUZZLE 68

Can you find your way through this circular maze, entering at the top and exiting at the bottom?

Entrance

Exit

PUZZLE 69

Remove two matchsticks to leave exactly two squares. Don't move any of the other matchsticks!

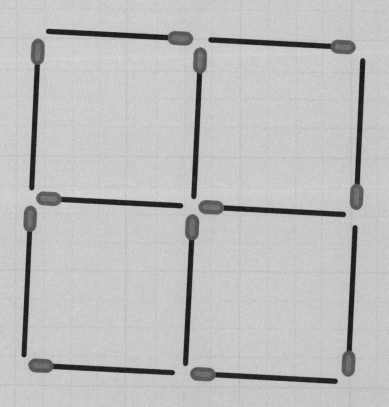

PUZZLE 70

How quickly can you solve this Brain Chain? Start with the number on the left, then apply each maths operation in turn. What is the final result?

RESULT

| 11 | X3 | +2 | -17 | X⅙ | -1 | ? |

I LIKE A BIT OF MATHS.

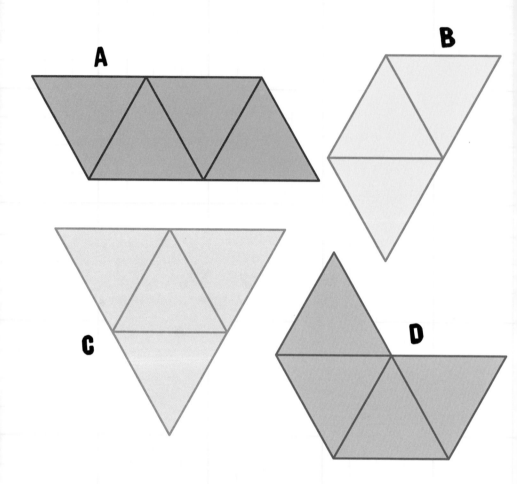

PUZZLE 71

Some of these shapes can be cut out and then folded along the lines to make a perfect four-sided pyramid. Without actually cutting them out, can you work out which ones won't fold to make a four-sided pyramid?

PUZZLE 72

Place one to six once each into every row, column and bold-lined area of the grid. All pairs of squares with a V between them must add up to 5, and all pairs of squares with an X between them must add up to 10.

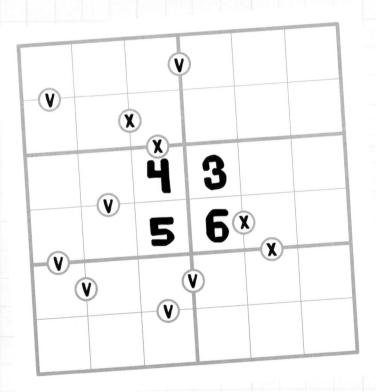

PUZZLE 73

Look at this set of shapes for 30 seconds, then cover them with a piece of paper or another book. Now draw out as many as you can remember on a separate piece of paper, in the same order. Once you've done that, uncover the page and see how many you remembered both correctly and in the correct position.

OOH, TRICKY ONE!

PUZZLE 74

By adding together two or more of these floating numbers, can you make all of the different totals below? Each floating number can only be used once per total.

20

32

24

31

22

23

9

40 60 88 100

PUZZLE 75

Imagine drawing along the grid lines. Can you work out how to divide this picture up into four identical shapes? Each grid square forms part of one of the four shapes, and none of the shapes overlap. You can rotate the shapes so they look the same, but you can't flip them.

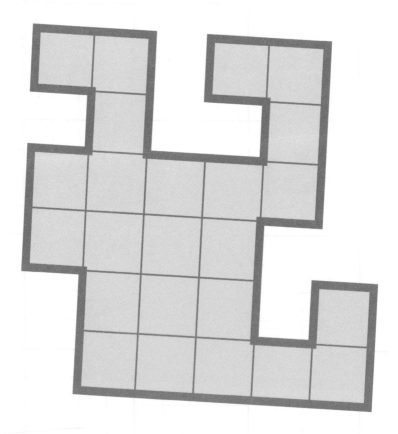

PUZZLE 76

Can you work out what shape would be revealed if you were to draw lines to join up all of the dots next to multiples of 7 in numerical order, starting at the lowest and finishing at the highest?

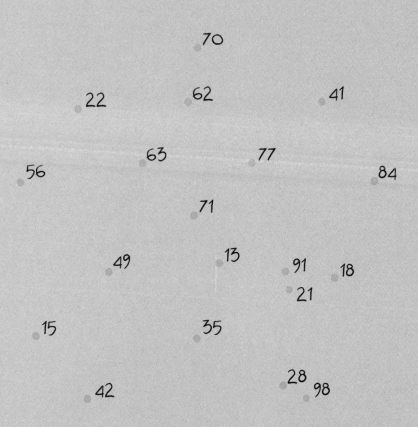

70

22　　　62　　　　　41

63　　　　77

56　　　　　　　　　84

71

49　　　13　　91　　18

21

15　　　35

28

42　　　　98

PUZZLE 77

Imagine cutting out and then rearranging these
tiles into a 2 x 3 grid, to reveal a number.
What number would it be?

PUZZLE 78

Fill each empty square with a letter from A to F,
so that each row, column and bold-lined shape
contains each letter exactly once.

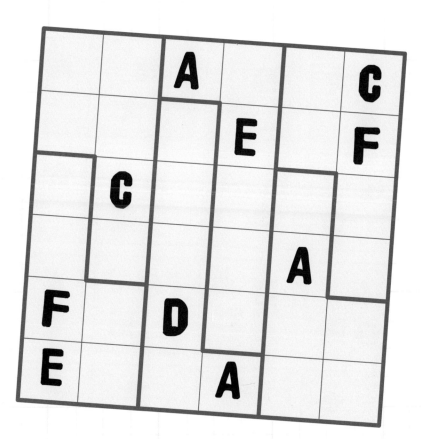

PUZZLE 79

Most, but not all, of these boxes contain different sets of shapes. How many pairs of boxes containing identical symbols can you find?

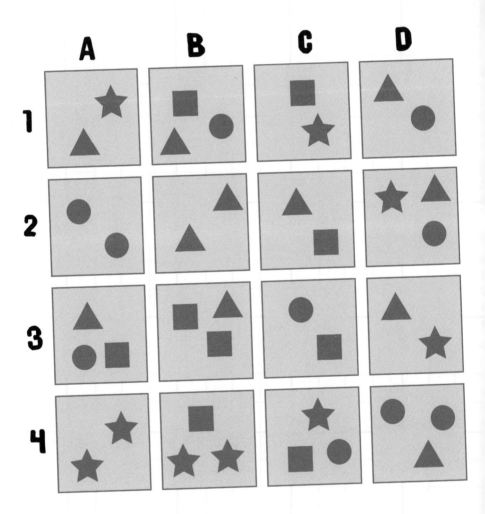

PUZZLE 80

Can you find your way through this maze,
entering at the top and exiting at the bottom?
Some paths cross over and under each other,
using the marked bridges.

Entrance

Exit

PUZZLE 81

Each day this week I have eaten twice as many sweets as I did the previous day. On Thursday I ate eight sweets. How many sweets did I eat in total from Monday to Friday this week?

YOU'RE GETTING GOOD AT THIS!

PUZZLE 82

How many cubes can you count in this drawing? Don't forget to count the 'hidden' ones at the back that must be holding up the cubes above them!

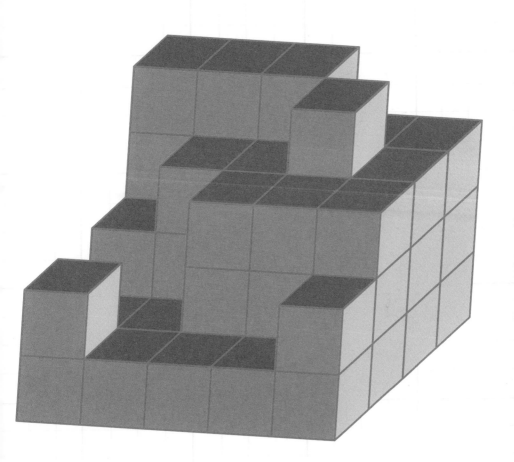

PUZZLE 83

If you were to rotate each image, A to C, as shown in the arrow beneath each image, which of the options, 1 to 3, would result in each case?

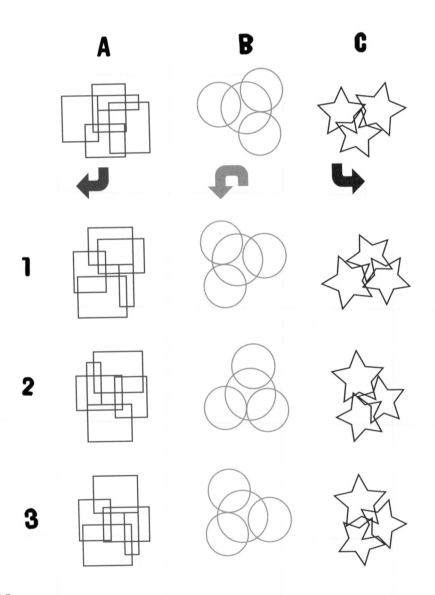

TEACHER

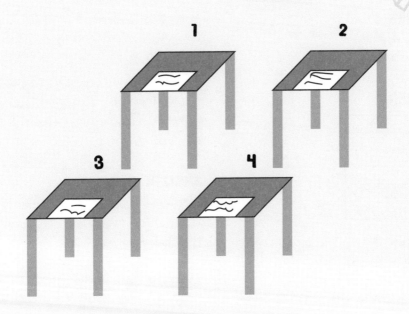

PUZZLE 84

Four pupils are sitting at desks, facing their teacher, in the positions numbered 1 to 4 in the picture. Can you work out who is sitting in which position?

* Daisy and Willow are sitting on different ends of different rows.
* Emma is sitting in the row furthest from the teacher, in either position 3 or position 4.
* Daisy is sitting to the left of Ava, in the same row.

ANSWERS

LEVEL A: SUPER BRAIN

ANSWER 1
A: 2 x 4, then + 1
B: 3 + 3, then x 2.

ANSWER 2

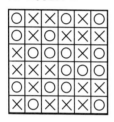

ANSWER 3
14 = 8 + 4 + 2
23 = 8 + 3 + 12
30 = 8 + 9 + 13.

ANSWER 4
30 – the difference between numbers increases by 1 at each step.

ANSWER 5
12.

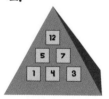

ANSWER 6
V.

ANSWER 7
5 or more letters is good; 7 or more is excellent; 9 is amazing!

ANSWER 8
D – the sequence reads square, circle, triangle, star and then repeats, reading left–to–right and row–by–row.

ANSWER 9
12 cubes: there are 9 cubes on the bottom layer and 3 cubes on the layer above.

ANSWER 10
A: 3 coins. 5p + 2p + 1p
B: 4 coins. 20p + 10p + 5p + 2p.

ANSWER 11
First scale: circle weighs the same as a square.
Second scale: square weighs the same as two triangles, which means a circle must also weigh the same as two triangles. Replacing the circle from the bottom scale with two triangles gives you option B.

ANSWER 12
There are 16 rectangles and squares. Don't forget, some of them overlap or are made up of more than one shape.

ANSWER 13
5 or more numbers is good;
7 or more numbers is excellent;
9 is incredible!

ANSWER 14
Shadow C.

ANSWER 15
5.

| 19 | 37 | 18 | 6 | 23 | 5 |

ANSWER 16
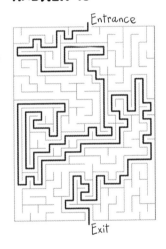

ANSWER 17
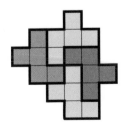

ANSWER 18

A	E	B	C	D
D	C	A	B	E
C	B	E	D	A
E	D	C	A	B
B	A	D	E	C

ANSWER 19
A1, B2, C3.

ANSWER 20
10 = 4 + 6
16 = 7 + 9
22 = 6 + 7 + 9
30 = 6 + 7 + 8 + 9.

ANSWER 21
A five-pointed star.

ANSWER 22
6 ways to get a total of 7: 1 + 6,
2 + 5, 3 + 4, 4 + 3, 5 + 2, 6 + 1.
3 ways to get a total of 4: 1 + 3,
2 + 2, 3 + 1.

ANSWER 23
4 or more shapes remembered and in the same position is good; 6 is excellent; all 7 is amazing!

ANSWER 24
1: Driving Cars; 2: All About Me; 3: Baking For Fun.

ANSWER 25
1 pair: A1 – B3.

ANSWER 26
x 2.

ANSWER 27
A) 22: 6 + 6 + 5 + 5
B) 14: 4 + 6 + 3 + 1.

ANSWER 28
An octagon.

ANSWER 29
There are 4 stars, 6 squares and 2 circles.

LEVEL B: MEGA MIND

ANSWER 30
Remembering 4 or more words is good; 6 or more is excellent; all 8 is fantastic!

ANSWER 31
1B, 2C, 3A.

ANSWER 32
x 3 and + 1.

ANSWER 33
24 = 8 + 16
33 = 16 + 17
42 = 8 + 16 + 18
55 = 10 + 11 + 16 + 18.

ANSWER 34

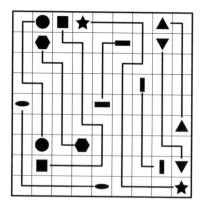

ANSWER 35

| 7 | 18 | 3 | 24 | 4 | 5 |

ANSWER 36
12 circles.

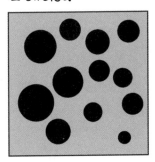

ANSWER 37
256 – the number doubles at each step.

ANSWER 38

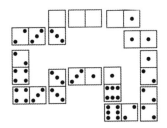

ANSWER 39
6 in the correct position is great; 8 is fantastic; and all 10 is excellent!

ANSWER 40
A: 88p. 50p + 20p + 10p + 5p + 2p + 1p.
B: 4 coins. You are owed 34p change (2 x 50p − 66p), made up of 20p + 10p + 2p + 2p.

ANSWER 41

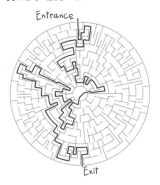

Entrance

Exit

ANSWER 42
Shape 1 – this has 4 sides, but all the other shapes have 5 sides.

ANSWER 43
A) 30: 6 + 6 + 6 + 6 + 6.
B) 18: 2 + 6 + 4 + 4 + 2.

ANSWER 44
6 in the correct position is great; 8 is fantastic; and all 11 is incredible!

ANSWER 45
The circle is heaviest; the triangle is lightest.

ANSWER 46

	2				1
0			5	3	1
	3	5		2	0
2				4	1
	3	4			2
		1	2		

ANSWER 47
A) 2 + 2, then x 2, then + 1.
B) 4 x 3, then – 2, then + 1
or 4 – 1, then x 3, then + 2.

ANSWER 48
29 = 14 + 8 + 7
39 = 14 + 18 + 7
48 = 14 + 18 + 16.

ANSWER 49
Seven sides.

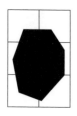

ANSWER 50

F	A	C	E	B	D
B	E	D	A	F	C
D	F	B	C	E	A
A	C	E	F	D	B
E	D	A	B	C	F
C	B	F	D	A	E

ANSWER 51
N – the sequence is capital letters which do not contain any curves, in alphabetical order.

ANSWER 52

ANSWER 53
22.

ANSWER 54
45 minutes: 5 + 10 + 30.

ANSWER 55
A – each diagonal (reading down and then across to the right) increases by 2 at each step.

ANSWER 56

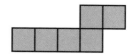

ANSWER 57

13:30 + 07:15 = **20:45**   20:10 – 07:10 = **13:00**
16:40 + 02:45 =**19:25**   09:20 – 02:30 = **06:50**
23:10 – 14:05 = **09:05**   03:25 – 02:15 = **01:10**
17:30 – 08:15 = **09:15**   10:40 + 10:00 = **20:40**
21:30 – 20:30 = **01:00**   04:05 + 05:05 = **09:10**
00:15 + 06:30 = **06:45**   18:55 – 07:25 = **11:30**
08:25 – 02:00 = **06:25**   15:30 + 04:00 = **19:30**
09:45 – 00:05 = **09:40**   01:15 + 05:00 = **06:15**

ANSWER 58
There are 20 rectangles and squares.

LEVEL G: ULTRA GENIUS

ANSWER 59
A) 7 + 2, then x 5, then – 4.
B) 8 x 3, then – 6, then + 7.

ANSWER 60

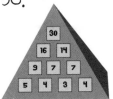

ANSWER 61
30.

ANSWER 62
55 – each number is equal to the sum of the two previous numbers.

ANSWER 63
H.

ANSWER 64
There are 31 rectangles and squares.

ANSWER 65
5 or more numbers is good;
7 or more numbers is excellent;
9 is incredible!

ANSWER 66
N, for 'nine' – they are the first letters of the numbers, starting at 1.

ANSWER 67
Shadow D.

ANSWER 68

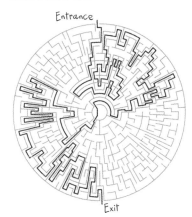

ANSWER 69

ANSWER 70

| 11 | 33 | 35 | 18 | 3 | 2 |

ANSWER 71

95

ANSWER 72

3	5	1	4	2	6
2	4	6	5	1	3
6	2	4	3	5	1
1	3	5	6	4	2
4	1	3	2	6	5
5	6	2	1	3	4

ANSWER 73

5 or more shapes remembered and in the same position is good; 7 or more is excellent; all 11 is amazing!

ANSWER 74

40 = 9 + 31
60 = 9 + 20 + 31
88 = 9 + 23 + 24 + 32
100 = 22 + 23 + 24 + 31.

ANSWER 75

ANSWER 76

A five-pointed star.

ANSWER 77

A number '2'.

ANSWER 78

B	E	A	F	D	C
A	D	C	E	B	F
D	C	E	B	F	A
C	F	B	D	A	E
F	A	D	C	E	B
E	B	F	A	C	D

ANSWER 79

2 pairs: A1 – D3 and A3 – B1.

ANSWER 80

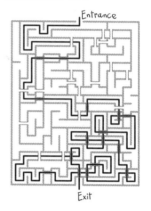

ANSWER 81

31 sweets: 1 on Monday, 2 on Tuesday, 4 on Wednesday, 8 on Thursday and 16 on Friday.

ANSWER 82

51 cubes: there are 20 cubes on the bottom layer, 15 cubes on the layer immediately above, 12 cubes on the layer above that, and 4 cubes on the top layer.

ANSWER 83

A3, B3, C2.

ANSWER 84

1: Daisy; 2: Ava; 3: Emma; 4: Willow.